First World War
and Army of Occupation
War Diary
France, Belgium and Germany

15 DIVISION
45 Infantry Brigade,
Brigade Trench Mortar Battery
24 November 1915 - 31 August 1916

WO95/1947/4

The Naval & Military Press Ltd
www.nmarchive.com
Published in association with The National Archives

Published by

The Naval & Military Press Ltd

Unit 10 Ridgewood Industrial Park,

Uckfield, East Sussex,

TN22 5QE England

Tel: +44 (0) 1825 749494

www.naval-military-press.com

www.nmarchive.com

This diary has been reprinted in facsimile from the original. Any imperfections are inevitably reproduced and the quality may fall short of modern type and cartographic standards.

© **Crown Copyright**
Images reproduced by permission of The National Archives, London, England, 2015.

Contents

Document type	Place/Title	Date From	Date To
Heading	1947/7 45th Brigade Trench Mortar Battery		
Heading	15 Div. 45 Bde 45 Trench Mortar Bty 1915 Nov To 1916 Aug.		
War Diary	36 NW Sheet 2 C 23 a.9.6	24/11/1915	24/11/1915
War Diary	36 NW Sheet 2 C17.a.1.3	24/11/1915	24/11/1915
War Diary	C 16d. 7.8.	25/11/1915	25/11/1915
War Diary	C17a.1.2.3	25/11/1915	25/11/1915
War Diary	1/C17a.1.3 2/C16 D.7.8	27/11/1915	27/11/1915
War Diary	Left Sector	06/12/1915	13/12/1915
War Diary	In The Field	12/12/1915	31/12/1915
Heading	45 Trench Motar Bty Jan 1916 Vol III		
War Diary	Sheet 36 C17C	08/01/1916	08/01/1916
War Diary	C.17C	09/01/1916	17/01/1916
War Diary	Sheet 36 C17C	18/01/1916	31/01/1916
War Diary	Sheet 36. C10.6.1.O	19/01/1916	19/01/1916
War Diary	In The Field C.10.d.5.6.	01/02/1916	28/02/1916
Heading	Confidential War Diary of 45. Trench Mortar Battery 1/7/16 To 31/7/16 (Volume)		
War Diary	Hohenzollern Section	01/07/1916	05/07/1916
War Diary	Goznay	06/07/1916	12/07/1916
War Diary	Hulluch Section	13/07/1916	21/07/1916
War Diary	Hoeux	22/07/1916	22/07/1916
War Diary	Tangry	22/07/1916	26/07/1916
War Diary	Nouvelle An Convet	26/07/1916	26/07/1916
War Diary	Beauvoir	27/07/1916	27/07/1916
War Diary	In Renault	28/07/1916	29/07/1916
War Diary	Vignacourt	31/07/1916	31/07/1916
Heading	Confidential War Diary of 45th Trench Mortar Battery. From 1st To 31st August 1916		
War Diary	Vignacourt	01/08/1916	02/08/1916
War Diary	Molliens Au Bois	03/08/1916	03/08/1916
War Diary	Bresle	04/08/1916	05/08/1916
War Diary	Trenches	07/08/1916	14/08/1916
War Diary	Albert	15/08/1916	18/08/1916
War Diary	Trenches	19/08/1916	31/08/1916

10/7/14

45th Brigade Trench Mortar Battery

~~2 Army Troops~~
15 DIV. 45 Bde

45

TRENCH MORTAR
BTY

1915 NOV TO 1916 AUG

(1643)

WAR DIARY or INTELLIGENCE SUMMARY

Army Form C. 2118

(Erase heading not required.)

Place	Date	Hour	Summary of Events and Information	Remarks and references to Appendices
36NW Sh.2. C17a.9.6.	29/11/15	2pm	The 4" gun was put in action in front of Potts Farm & Carnoy Rd. was fired. The obj. of firing to annoy an A.A. defence target presumed to self in the farm in the enemy's line about the position to hit this and sweep the shambles across it. The shooting was observed to be successful & about 60 rounds fired. Gun on target – no hostile fire range was about 3500yds. Enemy started search for war – cut rhythmic	Fired 86
36NW Sh.2. C17a.1.3.	"	3.45pm	Gun 4/pdr was active. Fired 88 rounds on enemy war trenches & rifle ranges, air shell hurried this it across trenches after this firing ceases in light no has	
C16.d.7.8	23/11/15	7pm	4" gun in action from a position in support lines (89,Skink) 8 rounds were fired into known Q Baraceae and damage was seen	
C17a.1.3.	"	9pm	to building a some. Two 4pdrs were brought into action & the assault of after 60 kamera visible to the list and 20 rounds were fired from position two 4pdrs took 88 rounds and reports were observed at Carnoy	
C17a.1.3. C16.D.7.8	29/11/15	3.15pm	Combined artillery & mortar action bef.2/Dec One 2"gun & One 1/2 gun were Mr. hyd. fires to destroy Lichy's M.G.M at head 8,C. 30 rounds were fired from gun and gun	(continues)

WAR DIARY
or
INTELLIGENCE SUMMARY

(Erase heading not required.)

Army Form C. 2118

L/o 5th T.M. Battery

Place	Date	Hour	Summary of Events and Information	Remarks and references to Appendices
Left Sector	Dec 6 to 13	6/30 am to noon 12.30 to 4 pm	Making Gun Emplacements & Dugouts in Reserve Trenches. Drawing & repairing trenches & Gun Emplacements previously made. No firing took place, & the above work was carried on daily throughout the week. The Gun detachments "Stand to" at Sunrise & Dawn when the Infantry Stand to.	

J. H. Didler 2/L
4.5th Trench Mortar Batty.

N 19/12

E.D.R.

WAR DIARY
or
INTELLIGENCE SUMMARY

Army Form C. 2118

Place	Date	Hour	Summary of Events and Information	Remarks and references to Appendices
			½ g" two planes on fuze head (99) d 2" n support head (88). Considerable damage was caused by 2" and 4 mortars, by the 7½ mm. There has been very effective shooting. 66% duds, when difficult for direct damage, although some of course hit rear trenches.	

A J Whelan 2nd Lt.
Or 45" Trench Mortar "B.g"

WAR DIARY or INTELLIGENCE SUMMARY

Army Form C. 2118

45th Trench Mortar Bde.

Place	Date 1915 Dec.	Hour	Summary of Events and Information	Remarks and references to Appendices
Kemmel	12th, &, 18th		Work on emplacements dug-out + bomb stores	Ag 1/16
	19th	3.30pm	Fired ten 4"dia bombs into enemy trenches in reply to the enemy trench mortars. All detonated.	
	20th, &, 21st		Work on emplacement, dug-out, bomb stores. Gully rd & walks do. All trenches flooded.	
	22nd	11.10am	Fired 30 rounds from Trench 88. 15 fired 2" & 15 fired 1½" Keep account shortly on acct of food beds. All detonated well & did considerable damage. Retaliation consisted of two Minenwerfer bombs, which did no damage.	
	23rd, &, 26th		Work on emplacements etc.	
	28th		Carried 25 D.M. Mortars with one 2" & 1½" in Ploegsteert woods. Started heavy practice on the 26. & completed same on rearmament of Brig 2pm on 11-2" mort[ar]s.	
	27th	2.55pm	Fired 26 rounds from Trench 119, 19 × 1½" & 17 × 2" short length 2" very good but with the 1½ only fair. Owing to the Berg Sponges habit	Old Hoy 2/Lt RFA OC 45H T.M.B.

WAR DIARY
or
INTELLIGENCE SUMMARY

(Erase heading not required.)

Army Form C. 2118

45th Trench Mortar Bty

Place	Date	Hour	Summary of Events and Information	Remarks and references to Appendices
In the field	27th	3.30pm	The soil to that line in which I prepared foundations affords but few rounds the enemy started search for the position. In spite of their very heavy shellfire & the firing of this gun from same emplacement in action for the scheduled hour, two men were recommended for cooking. One corporal was wounded. Work on emplacement kept stores etc.	
	28th to 3rd			

J Wilson 2/Lt RFA
OC 45th Trench Mortar Bty

4 & 5 Indian Motor Bde

Jan 1916
Vol III

Army Form. C. 2118

WAR DIARY
or
INTELLIGENCE SUMMARY   L/5 T.T. Trench Mortar Bty
(Erase heading not required.)

Place	Date	Hour	Summary of Events and Information	Remarks and references to Appendices
Sheet 36 C.17.c	Jan 1st 8th		Reconnoitring of emplacements etc.	
C.17.c 21.B.Z	9th	2:30pm	Fired 12 33/4" bombs at enemy's head.	
"	11th	11 A.M.	26 rounds new fuses from the 2" gun. 25 " " " " 3" ". In the action much damage was done to shelters, being very accurate.	
"	14th	2pm	20 rounds new fuses from the 2" gun. 45 rounds from the 4" M. There was a number of no touch with the 2" bombs.	
	15th 16th		Work on emplacement etc.	
C.17.c	17th		10 rounds new fuses from the 2" at the Bavarian S direct hits new trenches.	

A.F. Wilson 2/Lt 2 R.I.L.
0645 – 11 Nov 16

Army Form. C. 2118

WAR DIARY
or
INTELLIGENCE SUMMARY
(Erase heading not required.)

4/5th Bn Black Watch(?) T.F. Bde(?)

Place	Date	Hour	Summary of Events and Information	Remarks and references to Appendices
Sheet 36 C 17 c.	Jan 18-21	—	Work on dug-out & emplacements.	
"	22nd	12 pm	35 rounds were fired fr 2" gun, at enemy transport train.	
"	23rd	12.50 pm	Aeroplane was operation order 35 rounds were fired from h 2" gun.	
"	24th	1.30 pm	Aeroplane Co-operation order. 41 rounds from h 2" gun. 48 rounds were fired from h 1½ gun. 46 rounds from h 4 pm	
"	25th – 31st		Working on emplacements new roads, "Saturday" hornbeam etc.	

J. Hobson 9/11/1914
A/4-5" 7M B

Army Form. C. 2118

WAR DIARY
or
INTELLIGENCE SUMMARY 45th "Rough Riders" Bde
(Erase heading not required.)

Place	Date	Hour	Summary of Events and Information	Remarks and references to Appendices
Mont 6.19. C.6.i.a.	6.19		One detachment of 2" gun [struck out] were later from the 45th YM Bty. & One detachment of 1½" gun from the 42nd YM Bg. to ind-action at De Goyset with the 28 M Bat Fren at Morbin. Two days proven to action went away Systems emplacement & at 12.30 pm M.T. 1.9 M Bat. of cenad fire, new entry action at 4.44 pm Go rounds near Juesthen M. T.2' gm + 50 round from M. 2". The 2" detachment - 7th 45th Bg - was also kept there 7M gun. 7m 80th Bg - in action for some while.	

J.W. Wilson Mitchell
Lt. Col. 45th YM Bg.

45th Heavy Artillery Battery

Army Form C. 2118.

WAR DIARY
or
INTELLIGENCE SUMMARY
(Erase heading not required.)

Vol IV

Place	Date	Hour	Summary of Events and Information	Remarks and references to Appendices
In Field C.16.b.5. X	1.2.16	4.30pm	The 3.7" O.T.L. was taken into action as guard of Hythe. Installed against Boesch rifle grenades, four rounds were fired & successfully put a stop to the grenade. The 3.7 was again put in action & four rounds were fired.	
	8.2.16	4.15	The 1.5" was taken into action & 15 rounds were fired at Pont Ballot subject of hostile trench cutting successfully carried out.	
	2.2.16	12.30	Same target as before 15 rounds from 1½" & 15 rounds from 2" howr. of same successfully done.	
	11.2.16	3pm	The 2" howr was again in action & 12 rounds were fired at trenches trench cutting at C.17.c.	
	9.2.16	11AM	The 1.5" howr from 15"-1½" howr rounds 6.3.7" howr were 15" & 2" howr. The 1½" & 3.7" were fired at hostile modes successfully. Silencing same & the 2" was again now for cutting wire and cutting was done.	

T2134. Wt. W708-776. 500000. 4/15. Str J.C. & S.

WAR DIARY
or
INTELLIGENCE SUMMARY.
(Erase heading not required.)

Army Form C. 2118.

45th Canadian Howitzer Bty.

Place	Date	Hour	Summary of Events and Information	Remarks and references to Appendices
In the field B.56 C.16.	16/2/16	11.50 AM	Pt. Boesinghe Salient — our guns subjected to heaviest by 2" - 1½" 20 rounds & 15 rounds respectively. Much damage was done.	
	19/2/16	11 AM	Again Pt. Boesinghe Salient on trenches with 27 rounds 9½"	
	20/2/16	12.30 PM	Pt. ½" again fires 20 ½" rounds at enemy. Parapet & trenches excellent shots.	
	24/2/16	1 PM	Fired 30 rounds from 1½" for hostile flank during enemy attack.	
	29/2/16	12 N	Fired 2 ½" bursts from howitzers harrying offensive for a union infantry attack.	
	6/3/16	3 PM	Fired 40 rounds H.E. from Church St. installation to Boesche R/Q Granade fire — successful in stopping it.	

O.C. 45th Canadian Howr Bty.

Confidential

War Diary
of
45. Heavy Motor Battery

1/7/16 To 31/7/16

(Volume) -

WAR DIARY
INTELLIGENCE SUMMARY

Army Form C. 2118.

45th L. Mortar Battery

Place	Date	Hour	Summary of Events and Information	Remarks and references to Appendices
Hohenzollern Section	July 1st		Fighting Strength — Off 4, O.R. 41	
	5th		Relieved by 44th Light Mortar Battery. Relief complete by 6 P.M. Personnel proceeded to the Hill House, Gosnay, as billets.	
Gosnay	6th		Men rested and cleaned up.	
	8th		Lt Morrison and 2/Lt Robinson attended lecture at Sailly Labourse on "Interpretation of Air Photograph."	
	9-12		Fighting Strength: Off 4 O.R. 46. Men dug emplacements for Stokes mortars from Corps drawing. Planned work for gun teams.	
Hulluch Section	13th		45th L.M.B. relieved 44th L.M.B. in Hulluch Section	
	15th		Fighting Strength Off 4, O.R. 46	
	18th		Assisted 47th Bgde. raid on our right by bombarding Estelé salient G.12.D.52.8.	
	20th		Battery previous to raid by 6/7 R.S.T. bombarded G.12.D.52.8 with 11 Stokes mortars. Enemy left their trenches. Raid a failure.	
	21st		Unexpectedly relieved by 119th L.M.Batty. Proceeded to billets in Rue D'Heren Avenue Leo Aviens.	

WAR DIARY or INTELLIGENCE SUMMARY.

Army Form C. 2118.

(Erase heading not required.)

Instructions regarding War Diaries and Intelligence Summaries are contained in F.S. Regs., Part II. and the Staff Manual respectively. Title pages will be prepared in manuscript.

Place	Date	Hour	Summary of Events and Information	Remarks and references to Appendices
Hoeres	July 22nd		Marched with Brigade. Billeted at Tangry. Billets excellent. Fighting Strength 5 Off. 114 O.R. 4 H.	
Tangry Houvelle	23-25		Weather excellent. Practised men in open warfare tactics, and attacks on village.	
au Comte	26		Proceeded to billets here.	
Beauvois	27		do. Weather still very warm.	
Mt Renault	28		Proceeded to billets at Mt Renault Farm. Billets excellent. Conference of O.C. at 9pde HA attend. Re-billet. at 5.30 P.M. Tactics and organisation discussed. One given to battery for carrying purposes. Carrying party now 40 men. Lodged complaint that Randents were unsuitable as transport carts showing signs of wear. Wheels buckling etc.	
do	29th		G.O.C. 145th I.B. inspected battery in open tactics. Men engaged swim in river near Beaumont. Fighting Strength 5 Off. 4 O.R. 114.	
Vignacourt	31st		Marched at 4 A.M. to Vignacourt. Everybody pleased with early marching. Shad billets with 145th Machine Gun Company.	

H. Gardner Capt.
O.C. 145th L.M. Batty.

CONFIDENTIAL.

WAR DIARY

of

45th TRENCH MORTAR BATTERY.

From 1st to 31st AIGUST 1916.

VOLUME 2

Army Form C. 2118.

WAR DIARY
or
INTELLIGENCE SUMMARY.
(Erase heading not required.)

45th Light Mortar Battery

Instructions regarding War Diaries and Intelligence Summaries are contained in F.S. Regs., Part II. and the Staff Manual respectively. Title pages will be prepared in manuscript.

Place	Date	Hour	Summary of Events and Information	Remarks and references to Appendices
Vignacourt	1st Aug		Open warfare tactics practiced. Competition organised among gun teams in digging in.	
	2nd		Reconnoitred ground E of ALBERT.	
Millencourt	3rd		Billetted here for one day. Billets very poor. Weather still very warm.	
Bois	4th			
Breile	5th		Billets for men only fair, officers in tents.	
do.	6th		Reconnoitred G.O.C. 45th S.B. on his tour round front held by 69th Infy Bgde.	
			Fighting Strength Off. 4 O.R. 46.	
			Relieved 69th T.M.B. in Left Sector of Left Sector, III Corps. Good relief.	
Trenches	7th		45th S.B. relieved 69th S.B.	
do	8th			Fighting Strength Off. 4 O.R. 45
do.	12th		Assisted in attack by 6th Cam. Hrs & 6/7th R.S.F. in attack on GERMAN SWITCH.	
			Attack successful. Succeeded in our mission very to keep down machine guns on left	
do	14th		Relieved at 4 A.M. by 114th L.M.B. Proceeded to bivouac midway between	
			ALBERT and BECOURT WOOD.	
ALBERT	15th -18th		Weather very bad and bivouacs very uncomfortable. Men bathe very frequently in River ANCRE.	
	18th		Stood to arms twice this afternoon. Lt. Robinson goes to hospital	

Army Form C. 2118.

WAR DIARY
or
INTELLIGENCE SUMMARY.
(Erase heading not required.)

Instructions regarding War Diaries and Intelligence Summaries are contained in F. S. Regs., Part II. and the Staff Manual respectively. Title pages will be prepared in manuscript.

Place	Date	Hour	Summary of Events and Information	Remarks and references to Appendices
Trenches	19th Aug		Relieved 4th R.M.B. in right section. Left sector III Corps front. Fighting Strength Offrs 4. O.R. 45.	
do	20th		"Sniper" captured up to road. 1 Sgt. 1 man killed. 3 men wounded. Snipers taken out owing to lack of targets.	
do	22nd		Mortars (2) put in and trained on German INTERMEDIATE TRENCH.	
do	24		Assisted bombers of 6th Camerons in their attack on INTERMEDIATE TRENCH. Owing to our right unsuccessful. Prisoner captured said our mortar fire was very destructive to their morale, and had annihilated a whole platoon.	
do	26th		2 mortar party to 4th Army School of Instruction. Fighting Strength Offrs 4. O.R. 40	
do	27th		Only a small part of INTERMEDIATE TRENCH still occupied. Fired 154 rounds on it during the night.	
do	28th		Still continue to bombard INTERMEDIATE TRENCH heavily. Proposed attack cancelled.	
do	29th		Weather very bad. Received notification that P. Robison had been sent to England 20/8/16.	
	30th		Hostile garrison of INTERMEDIATE LINE surrenders. Trenches bad.	
	31st		Mortars now trained on BOTTOM TRENCH. Trenches very dirty.	

A Gardner Capt.

www.ingramcontent.com/pod-product-compliance
Lightning Source LLC
Chambersburg PA
CBHW081252170426
43191CB00037B/2127